My Sister, Orphan Annie

A Sister's Tribute

Helen Kominsky Frangos

ROZ MILLER

Disclaimer – this is a loving tribute by a younger sister to an older sister and the challenges each experienced in their lives.
Persons mentioned in this book are real people

Acknowledgements
Helen Kominsky Frangos' story
as told to and written by Roz Miller.
Media Masters Productions for consultation

Dedication

Dedicated to the memory of my parents,
my siblings, especially my sister, Annie.

About Orphans:

*"Just remember, you are never alone. There
is always someone who loves you, someone
who is rooting for you, and someone who
believes in you."*

Also, by *ROZ MILLER*

Trail of Tales – Rhyming Poetry Collection

Table of Contents

Chapter 1 – The Beginning

The bond between siblings is frequently silent and strong; especially between sisters. As one of eight siblings, I have now outlived them, all of them, but the memories linger in my mind and in my heart.

Our dad, Joseph Kominsky sailed from Poland for the United States in the early years of the twentieth century for a better life.

The German ship that brought him across the Atlantic Ocean discharged passengers at Ellis Island in New York Harbor.

Our mother, Anna Magas, grew up in a small Polish farm village, came to the United States with her Aunt Rose, when she was about fourteen-years-old. They brought enough food with them to last the ten-day steerage voyage on the German ship Kaiser Wilhelm. They were also processed into America through Ellis Island.

Established in 1902, Ellis Island in New York harbor was the facility through which all immigrants from Europe passed through to be accepted into the United States.

Today the 27.5-acre Ellis Island in Hudson County, New Jersey, houses the Ellis Island Immigration Museum and is accessible to the public only by guided tours and only by ferry. Since 1976, it is part of the National Park Service.

Now part of the Statue of Liberty National Monument, the United States Public Health Service hospital on Ellis Island was in service between 1902 and 1951. Contagious diseases were treated in a separate pavilion of the hospital.

Anna and Joesph were grateful to be healthy because if immigrants coming through Ellis Island were sick and not healthy, they were returned to their home country.

Anna left her parents and siblings behind in Poland, never to see them again. Written correspondence was by slow mail. She spoke only Polish, but knew she could and would learn to read, write and speak English. Years later, she became an American Citizen, as did Joesph.

After being accepted into the United States through Ellis Island, Anna was hired by a Polish Jewish couple in New York City to do domestic housework and because she spoke Polish. Also included in her duties was caring for the couple's small children.

Anna and Aunt Rose drifted apart and eventually lost touch with each other.

. . . . .

As young people, Anna and Joseph were both Catholic and they liked to dance. They met at a weekend dance held by a Catholic church in Manhattan.

Mom, Anna Magras, was sixteen years old when she married Joseph Kominsky, who was eighteen or nineteen years old.

Not wanting to live in New York City to begin their family, the young couple moved to Pennsylvania for Dad to work in the coal mines because the work was steady with good pay. A bit later, they moved to West Virginia to work in the coal mines. There was no union membership at the time. Dad had not realized how harsh work conditions would be in the West Virginia mines.

Not being able to stand erect, the miners had to bend over with lamps attached to their helmets so they could see to pick the coal which was then carted to the mine entrance. Coal picking was slow and hard. Miners were paid for the amount of coal they picked per day.

. . . . .

By the time Anna was in her early twenties, she and Joesph were parents of four children, Mary, Walter, Andrew, and Anna (Annie). They were followed by Emil, me–Helen, Irene, and Delores.

Not only were the work conditions harsh and challenging, so were the living conditions. Life in the mining camps was hard and difficult for the miners and their families. Mining camp life lacked the basics and made life more difficult. There was no indoor running water or indoor plumbing and no electricity. We burned wood for warmth, and the women cooked on wood-burning stoves. The laundry was done outdoors in washtubs with scrub-boards. The hand wrung wet laundry was hung on outdoor clotheslines to air-dry.

Chapter 2 – Sister Anna

Born in 1919, my older Sister, Little Anna, child number four, known throughout her life as Annie, was just two years old when she contracted polio. She received no medical treatment at that time because the family could not afford the treatment. The Salk polio vaccine was not developed for mass usage until April 1955.

7

Our Dad, known as Pappa Joesph, had been a carpenter apprentice in Poland, a skill he did not use in his new homeland. Pappa Joesph made a little wooden wagon so Annie's brothers could pull her about so she could join the childhood activities of her siblings. When she became school-age, her brothers would pull Annie in the little wagon to school and back home each day.

Concerned about Annie's well-being, her first-grade teacher called the crippled children's hospital in Columbus, Ohio, and told them about Annie's polio and home life situation. The hospital administration and medical team agreed to accept Annie as a patient.

Because of her lack of medical treatment when she contracted polio as a very young child and with no braces for walking, her legs had to be broken at the knees and reset to be put into a cast. Annie stayed at the children's hospital because at the time our parents could not adequately care for her at home in the Ohio coal mining camp. There was only a latrine for hygiene needs, there was no indoor running water or electricity. All the families in the mining camps were poor, and many were immigrants or blacks.

As Annie grew, her braces were adjusted to accommodate her growth. The support brace was padded at the hip, her shoes were 'high top' and attached to the braces which locked at the knees. New braces were provided by the county as Annie grew and developed.

After yet another move, Pappa Joseph and Anna, known in the family and friends as Bubka, went from West Virginia to Blaine, Ohio, an unincorporated community in Belmont County, Ohio, for work in the coal mine. After this move, they had three more children, Emil, me-Helen, Irene and Delores.

Chapter 3 – Children's Home

Built in 1880, the Belmont Children's Orphanage was in Barnesville in Belmont County, Ohio. The children's home was designed by the prominent Ohio architect, Joseph William Yost. Built on 65 acres with hilltop vistas, the acreage was purchased for five thousand dollars. The four-story building had a cupola on each of the central towers.

A county official, Mr. Conrow, visited the orphanage and stated, an orphanage is no place to put children. The name was changed to the Belmont Children's Home.

The children's home served the needs of children and their families in the surrounding area from its opening in 1880 until it closed in 1981, giving the children a safe and secure home run by a loving and caring staff.

Eventually all of us Kominsky siblings were sent to the Children's Home because our parents could not adequately care for us. Mom signed over our custody to the children's home. When we moved in, the orphanage required all the children to have their tonsils removed, and we did.

We received good care and discipline from Mr. and Mrs Gillispie,

Children's Home directors. They loved the children in their care. We learned many of life's basic lessons from the Gillispies and the attending staff. We adjusted quickly, and we loved the Children's Home. It was paradise to us, compared to our difficult life we had in the mining camp.

Belmont Children's Home – Barnesville, Ohio – 1880 - 1980

The Children's Home was self-sufficient. Under the guidance of Mr. Forrest, the boys did all the gardening. Vegetables grown in the garden were prepared by the kitchen cook-staff for us to eat.

The boys also took care of fruit orchards and tending the farm animals. Mr. Doudna helped the boys with the orchards. The chores and tasks performed by the children was part of our practical classroom education, teaching us skills while providing what we needed to survive. The vegetable farms, orchards, and dairy provided most of what we ate.

In addition to providing a safe facility and caring staff for the children living there, by being a self-sufficient institution, the children learned useful skills which served us throughout our lives.

We liked going to meals in the home's dining room. This was a special time during our day. We especially remember each table in the big dining room had large pitchers of fresh, cold milk from the farm's cows for us to drink. We had freshly baked bread and sweet butter churned from milk produced by the home's cows. We liked the aroma of freshly baked breads, cakes, and pies.

As the girls grew into their teens, we were assigned to assist with certain dining room chores. The boys helped in the kitchen.

Once, when I did not show up for supper, Annie asked one of the attendants where I was. After a search of the dormitory, I was found accidentally locked in a closet. Annie and I always looked out for each other.

Superintendent Gillispie had a separate dining room where influential dignitaries who could help the school were invited and entertained as mealtime guests.

Grade School was in the courtyard of the Children's Home. In the summer we went to school bare-foot and wore shoes only in the winter when it was cold. The shoes were donated by area families to the school for us to wear. Most everything the school had was donated; rocking chairs for the porch, furniture for all the dorm rooms, tables and chairs for the dining room, and clothing for us to wear. Area families saw that the center had what it needed to care for the children.

The big, two-story children's home had a tin roof. We would lie in our beds and listen to the rain hitting the roofs. We liked the sound, while it lolled us to sleep.

Every Sunday we all gathered for vespers to listen as the girls and boys sang hymns that drifted throughout the halls.

The young children loved the singing. We looked forward to the singing each week.

Mrs. Gillispie had two sons who became doctors and became life-long friends with my three brothers, Walter, Adnrew, and Emil, because they were all near the same age.

Mr. and Mrs. Gillispie would come to the children's home with penny candy from which we learned how to barter. There were times when they invited us to play in their beautiful fenced front yard of their home. These play times ended with the Gillispies serving us home churned ice cream as a Sunday afternoon treat.

Chapter 4 – Bubka Remarries

Annie was eleven years old when she came home from the hospital. Soon after her return Pappa Joseph died. I was about three years old. Mom knew without Pappa Joseph; she could not keep all her children and the family together and provide what they needed. She contacted the county officials. Because there was an orphanage nearby in Barnesville, Ohio, she sent all her children to the Belmont Children's Orphanage. Mom, who had no other place to go, went to the Belmont infirmary for immigrants. Our oldest sister became a live-in domestic nearby.

While Mom was in the poor house, Bubka's friends were concerned about her and her small children so they searched for a suitable man for Mom to marry.

Nicholas, also a miner, had empathy for Irene and me being in the Children's Home. He married Mom, and they took us back to the mining camp with them.

The mining camp was comprised of forty company houses. Half were occupied by black families and half by immigrant families, which we were.

Even as adults, we never forgot the summer nights when the KKK, on the hill behind our house, performed cross-burning ceremonies while wearing their white robes. That's why outsiders called our mine camp the PATCH, or little Africa.

Years later we learned some of the Klan were prominent men from the local area. We never let on that we knew who they were.

After experiencing the KKK activities, Annie was so frightened of the dark, it gave her nyctophobia. She always slept with the light on, even as an adult.

Being back home with Bubka and her new husband, Nicholas, did not work out well and certainly was not ideal for two little girls. Nicholas was not the caring stepfather Bubka wanted and expected. He could be quite verbally abusive. Irene and I welcomed being sent back to the Children's Home and avoid the verbal abuse.

At the children's home, as we grew, we were taught skills by the center's staff and given duties as our age and skills allowed. While at the children's home, Little Annie learned homemaking, sewing, and quilting skills. She was a quick learner and loved working with beautiful fabrics. She taught her fellow children the sewing skills she developed and enjoyed so much.

Annie was liked by everyone because she was always cheerful, had a bubbly personality, and had a positive outlook on life despite her polio affliction. She never allowed the polio to drag her down. Never a "Why me?"

· · · · ·

After learning President Franklin Delano Roosevelt had polio, Annie always wanted to visit Warm Springs, Georgia, where the President went for his polio treatments, but she could never afford to make the trip. This was one of her big disappointments and regrets in life.

Chapter 5   Domestic Skills

The Negus family, one of Belmont County's prominent families, lived in a big two-story Victorian house on acreage that had a large fruit orchard. The Negus family engaged Annie out of the children's home to take care of little Nancy, the Negus' young daughter, who was about five years of age.

Annie got little Nancy ready for bed. Then Annie would read stories to her.

Pauline, Annie's friend, was also engaged out to help in the Negus home. Pauline helped washing the fine China and crystal when it was used for fancy dinners for entertaining Negus' family, friends, and associates.

. . . . .

Annie's trustee from the Children's Home, Mr. Cox, came once a year to check how she was adjusting to her surroundings. Annie knew she could be more than a domestic helper for wealthy families. She told Mr. Cox she wanted to attend business school and learn the skills needed to become a secretary.

Annie remained at the children's home until she was twenty-one years old when Mr. Cox enrolled her in the Elliott Business School in the Hawley Building in

Wheeling, West Virginia. She lived just across the Ohio River in Martins Ferry, Ohio, and commuted to classes by bus.

Business school was a one-year program of education, preparing and developing skills needed for offices and businesses to run smoothly and effectively. While attending business school, Annie lived with the Dobbins family and helped with housework.

Annie especially liked bathing in the Dobbins' big tin bathtub, relaxing in the warm water. She had no difficulty getting into and out of the tub and could stand just long enough without the braces to take care of her personal needs.

Chapter 6   Washington DC

After Annie completed her one-year
course at the business school, Lawrence
E. Imhoff, was elected to the US House of
Representatives for Ohio's 18th District
from 1933 to 1939 and again from 1941 to
1943. Mr. Imhoff needed a secretary, so he
asked Mr. Cox for a recommendation. Mr.
Cox recommended Annie. She worked for

representative Imhoff during his time in
Washington, DC.

Annie Kominsky in Washington, DC

Annie's three close friends helped
her find an apartment in Washington. She
had no difficulty going up the steps, but the
process navigating the steps was slow.

She had to unlock her braces and hold onto the right arm-railing navigating the steps, then lock it again at the top or bottom of the stairs.

Living in Washington, there were many cultural activities available. Annie and her friends enjoyed weekend visits to area museums and art galleries. She especially liked visiting the Smithsonian Institution just off the mall.

. . . . .

Annie came to the coal mining camp in Ohio to visit Bubka and me. After getting off the bus, and transferring to a streetcar, we met Annie at the Iron Bridge after crossing the railroad tracks.

As we crossed the bridge, the local black, Preacher Thornebill, was baptizing some of his church members in the creek that was clear because it was the weekend and there was no collected debris in the creek. We all sang "Shall We Gather at the River" as we crossed the bridge.

We walked to the top of the hill where Bubka lived. The geese were out, and they liked to chase Annie because of her shiny metal braces.

To make a little extra money, each spring, Bubka would collect the goose down and make goose down pillows. Each quill had to be stripped to collect the down. Bubka had to be careful collecting the down because the soft, fine feathers would scatter like dandelions in a spring breeze.

After each of Annie's visits, she took the bus back to her apartment in Washington, DC.

Chapter 7   Wisconsin

When Congressman Imhoff's term was over, and he was not reelected, he told Annie about the nuns at the Winnebago Hospital in Wisconsin. She took the train to Oshkosh to live and work. Her nursing friends helped her prepare for departure and board the train. Mr. Imhoff contacted the hospital nuns. He was influential in getting Annie a job at the hospital doing secretarial work.

While working at the hospital, Annie started flirting with a hospital electrician. Her friends warned her he was engaged, and not to waste her time on him. But, with her compelling personality and winning smile, she won him over, braces and all. Annie and Frank Schrader were married at the Winnebago County courthouse in the late 1950s.

We enjoyed many dinners at Frank's parents' home in Wisconsin. After the meals, we sat on the porch sharing stories and experiences as we rocked in chairs brought over from Germany.

Frank's dad offered each of his three adult children five thousand dollars or a diamond of equal value. Ever thrifty Frank took the cash and used it as a down payment on a house for him and Annie.

Annie loved her home life, Frank, and her cat. She was a wonderful cook who loved inviting family and friends over to enjoy her home-cooked meals. We loved to sit on the back porch and socialize with family, friends, and neighbors.

Frank also liked working with his hands. He built and painted birdhouses for fun, giving them to family and friends. We put out bird seed to attract birds.

· · · · ·

An avid reader and a forever learner, Frank frequently got on his moped and rode to the library. Because he was very frugal, Frank always went to the library to read the Wall Street Journal rather than buying it. Annie knew Frank frequently liked going to the library, but she did not know his why for going. Frank's dad got him interested in investing. Frank read and studied financial publications as a secret investor.

One year when I was visiting Annie and Frank, he forgot and left his notebook on the couch. I saw his whole stock portfolio. His quiet, secret investing made him a very successful investor and a very wealthy man.

Creative, talented, and just as thrifty as Frank, Annie always sewed her own clothing. She never bought store-bought clothing. She liked to sew flared skirts to hide her braces and for comfort and ease of movement.

. . . . .

In 1964 Annie and Frank took a trip to the World's Fair in New York City's Queens borough. Frank drove six of us from Wisconsin to New York City to the fair in a little Chevy, no seat belts. We visited each country's pavilion, seeing the sights. We learned much about countries we would never be able to visit.

Annie especially enjoyed seeing the huge World's Fair Unisphere at the fair's entrance. The fair's theme was "Peace Through Understanding" and it was dedicated to "Man's Achievements on a Shrinking Globe in an Expanding Universe." The stainless-steel globe of the world was designed by Gilmore Clarke. It was constructed and installed by the American Bridge Company, a division of the US Steel company.

On the drive home, a couple of flat tires inconvenienced us and slowed us down. Two new tires and service added to our vacation expenses.

Chapter 8   Wrestler

Bobby Douglas, Olympic wrestler in 1964 and 1968, came to live with his grandmother Davis at the mining camp, when he was six-years-old. A poor, barefoot kid like us, Bobby became our playmate and our friend.

The second time around, stepping into a child-rearing role, Grandma Davis had a switch at the ready, as a reminder, just in case, But, Bobby was a good kid. He ran errands for his grandmother as needed and her neighbors when they need an assist.

Everyone took Bobby in and mentored him. Everyone loved Bobby. Annie knitted Bobby a toboggan hat that he liked so much, he wore it all winter and summer.

Bobby Douglas – our playmate and our life-long friend

Like many of our fellow mining camp neighbors, we raised chickens. As neighbors of Grandma Davis, our mother would chop off a chicken's head to cook it for supper. When Grandma Davis killed a chicken, she would ring its neck, then each would dunk the chicken into scalding hot water, pluck the feathers, dress it, and cook it using their very tasty home recipes for supper. We would help with the feather plucking.

Like most others in the mining camps, we continued to have small garden plots by our camp cottages. We all became master gardeners, following in our mother's footsteps. This was something we did to survive during the depression. Our garden vegetables were added to the chicken for a tasty meal.

. . . . .

Bobby began wrestling as a middle-school student. By the time he was in high school, he had competed in and had won enough matches, to receive many wrestling scholarships. He chose to attend Iowa State University in Ames.

Bobby had an illustrious life as a competing wrestler and was the first black wrestling college coach. His wrestling students participated in many Olympics and one of his students won an Olympic medal.

Douglas was honored two times as USA Wrestling Coach of the Year.

. . . . .

When Coach Bobby and his wrestling team were to attend the 2004 Olympics in Greece, my daughter, Melissa, then living in Greece, bought tickets for the wrestling events.

Melissa and Bobby messaged each other notes at the Olympics because it was the easiest way for them to communicate. Bobby coached Ciel Saunderson to an Olympic Gold Medal performance that year.

. . . . .

When the old Ironside Bridge needed to be replaced in Blaine, Ohio, the newly constructed bridge was renamed the Bobby Douglas Bridge. Many locals for miles around and all the area politicians and government officials attended the dedication of the new bridge. Folks from all over came for the dedication service.

Annie and Frank drove from Wisconsin for the dedication. My daughter, Melissa, and her young sons came from Greece where they were living, for the bridge dedication.

Bobby was so humbled by the many friends attending from all over the country and several from out of the country. By now, Grandma Davis was deceased, and Bobby had lost his mother.

Chapter 9   Auction

The Children's Home, after one hundred years of caring for children in need, in Barnesville, Ohio, was to be demolished in 1981. An auction was organized and held to raise funds for needy children in the area. Annie made sure she attended the auction. She wanted one of the big milk pitchers which sat on the dining room tables at mealtime.

People attended from all over the country, to bid on auction items. They were bidding on and buying a piece of their childhood lives. They were buying memories.

· · · · ·

A big enclosed glass museum display case in Barnesville had the names of all the children who had lived in the home and who also served in the military, including my three brothers.

Laid in 1879, the Children's Home cornerstone is now in the Watt Center for History and the Arts in Saint Clairsville, Ohio.

A children's cemetery remains on the site which is still maintained.

Chapter 10   Senior Residence

When Frank died at age eighty, my brother, Andrew, was the executor of Frank's will. Andrew moved Annie to Lakeside senior living center in Detroit, Michigan.

When we visited, Annie loved getting our sister Irene and me to dance with the residents at the senior living center. Annie could not dance but she loved watching folks dance the polka.

Annie was adept at making the best of a bad situation. She turned her handicap into an advantage. She'd get onto her scooter and navigated from the senior residence to the mall across the busy highway every Sunday to shop or just browse the latest merchandise in the stores. Her first stop was always to the fabric department.

When Irene and I visited Annie, the three of us would go to the Lakeside Mall. Annie loved buying fabric to sew more dresses. After lunch on our mall trips, Annie always liked to buy a bag of chocolates to share as a special treat.

Chapter 11   Final Curtain

My siblings and I were born to parents who left family behind in Poland for a new, better life in America. The streets were not paved with gold, but the freedom of opportunity was golden. Our parents fell short of their hopes and expectations. But, all the Kominsky siblings born into poverty, experienced the American Dream and did well. "That's America for you."

We knew we were loved during the difficult times we all shared. Life in the Children's Home was a blessing. In spite of our difficult childhood, we all became solid adults, appreciating the difficulties our parents endured helping us become the resilient adults we all became.

When Annie went to the Negus home, my brother, Andy, went into the CCC - Civilian Conservation Corps, President Roosevelt's work relief program (1933-1942 camps in Salt Lake City). Andy received thirty dollars per month from the CCC. He kept five dollars and sent twenty-five dollars to our parents. Through CCC, Andy learned useful skills for life.

The other two brothers joined the Army. Brother Walter was stationed at Pearl Harbor. Brother Emil won a Purple Hart for his service in Europe. After Andy left the CCC, he attended officer training school to become a captain. And, I, Helen, stood on my feet all day for forty years, making my hair salon clients more attractive.

All of the Kominsky siblings became solid citizens and successful adults. Two of us, Annie and I, because of our thrifty, hard-working husbands; Annie's as an electrician and mine as a steel mill worker, through their frugal investing, we became millionaires.

Our good friend, Nancy T. was the last child to leave the children's home. She went back many times because she had nowhere to go.

Nancy was always our friend, moral support, and encourager. "You can do it. Give it a try." Her positive attitude and encouragement were appreciated. It helped us to try and accomplish more.

When she met and married Mitch, they had a good life together as the parents of five children. Mitch once rode his bicycle from Washington State to New York City. Nancy followed him in her van.

During the years spent living at the Children's Home, Annie made many life-long friends. She stayed in touch with her friends with beautifully hand-written letters.

My belief is that there is no substitute for family. Parents are the glue that holds families together, good times and bad. Siblings are fortunate to have each other. It is a blessing to be a grandparent and great-grandparent.

Many things in life we have no control over, but we adapt to handle what life deals us. My siblings and I adapted well from our challenging and difficult childhood experiences. We were all born into poverty, but we all grew out of it.

Pappa Joseph was buried in a pauper's grave in a Catholic cemetery in Wheeling, West Virginia. Bubka was buried in a Catholic cemetery in Yorkville, Ohio.

Best lesson learned from Mom, love your family and keep it together as best you can. Frugal hard work makes one stronger to survive life's bumps. We leaped many bumps and hurdles during our lives, coming out stronger as a result.

Frank died at eighty years of age. Annie lived at the Lakeside care facility approximately ten years until her death in 2009 at the age of ninety, still wearing shoes with steel braces attached because of her polio. Annie was buried in Wisconsin next to Frank. Her last wish was to make and wear a white dress so St. Peter would let her enter through the Pearly Gates.

Cherish your family memories, write your stories, and share with your family and maybe the world as a gift to be passed down to succeeding generations. They will appreciate knowing about their family and you for saving, writing, and sharing your family stories with them.

I am ninety-seven years old as I tell this story. I have three daughters and eight grandchildren.

These are my memories, my story of my parents, my siblings and especially of my older sister, orphan Annie.

Made in the USA
Monee, IL
18 October 2024

67573525R00036